# Easy Rock 'n' Roll

## For Beginners

Southern House Publishing

ISBN: 978-1-9997478-8-6

tylermusic.co.uk

# CONTENTS

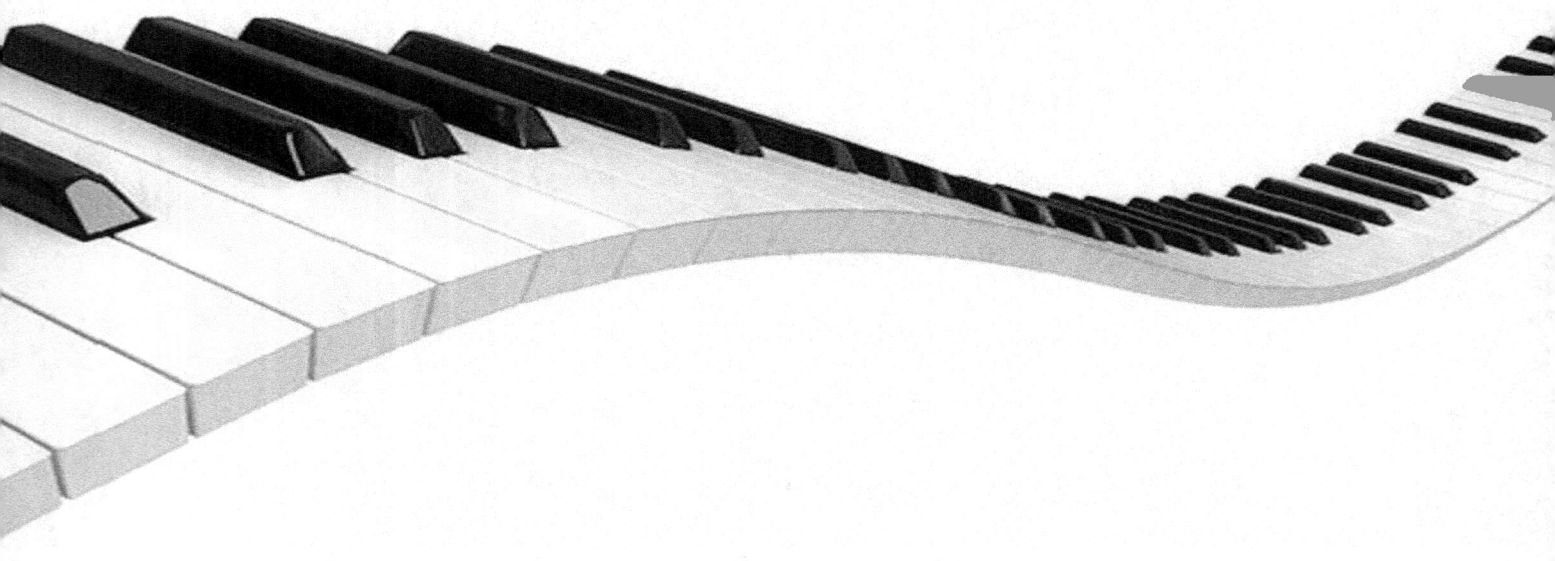

# Introduction

If you are reading this then you probably have an interest in learning to play rock 'n' roll piano, so I will start by congratulating you on having great taste in both music and also instruments. The energetic styles of the likes of Jerry Lee Lewis and Little Richard shook the world and influenced many musicians that followed. It might not be mainstream anymore, but it still has loyal followers, is great fun to play and what you learn can also be incorporated into other styles.

Rock 'n' roll developed in the United States and came of age during the 1950s. It arguably evolved primarily from the blues, although it was also influenced by country, gospel, and rhythm and blues, perhaps even some jazz artists also. Different influences can always be heard in the music of different artists. The style we concentrate on here could perhaps be referred to as rockabilly, although rock 'n' roll is all encompassing.

The purpose of this book is to give those that are new to playing rock 'n' roll piano a first step into the style. Its aim is to cover the basics and get you started, the examples begin easy and then gradually increase in difficulty while introducing a few extra elements along the way. Once you have the basics that this book provides, you'll be able to progress further with other publications of a higher difficulty level, using some of the sheet music that's available and hopefully from listening to the music too.

Thanks for reading this little intro, I hope you will find this book helpful on the start of your musical journey, and I further hope that you will continue on, helping to keep the music alive. But most of all, just enjoy it, it's what music was made for.

# Fingering Suggestions

The fingering suggestions within the book use the standard finger numbering system, meaning that both thumbs are counted as being number one with the little fingers being number five.

Being an introduction to rock'n'roll piano rather than an initial 'learn to read and play music' book, it's obviously necessary to have some basic knowledge of playing the piano. Some fingering suggestions are included for the left-hand patterns to help guide people in the right direction if they so desire, although they are only suggestions and alternatives can work in some instances.

## Finger Numbering

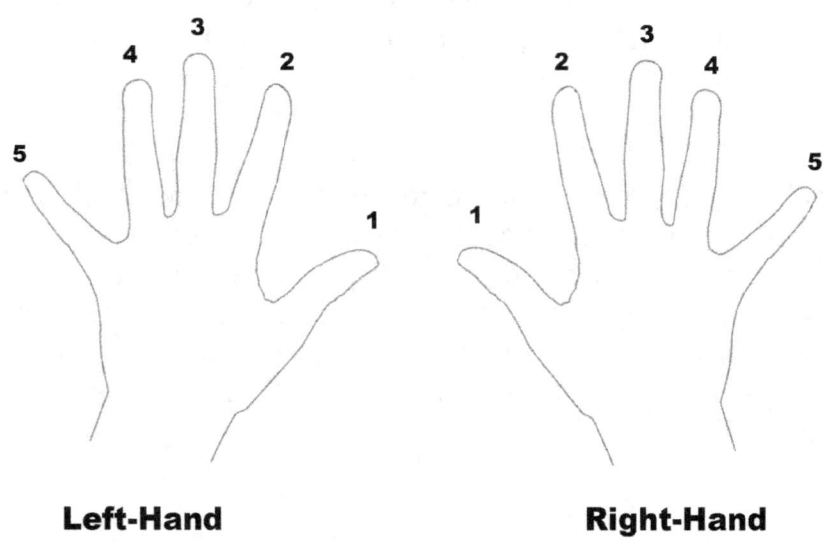

**Left-Hand**                    **Right-Hand**

## Audio Examples

The examples that have audio to accompany them, can be identified by having the relevant number next to an audio sign. For access, refer to page 71, for information regarding downloading them from the website.

**Example  Accompanying Audio Sign**

# Common Chord Progression

Rock 'n' roll uses various chord progressions, with possibly the most common being the twelve-bar blues progression. This isn't particularly surprising, seeing as the blues was partially responsible for its development.

The twelve-bar blues progression in its most basic form uses three chords, which makes it quite easy to remember. Its simplicity here is frowned upon by some, but it is part of what makes the music magical in my opinion.

The three chords used for traditional rock'n'roll, are commonly referred to as being the ONE – FOUR – FIVE chords. This is more simply and commonly written as the Roman numerals, I – IV – V.

You might have come across this before, but just in-case you are wondering what on earth I'm talking about, here's a brief explanation.

**The 'C' Major Scale**

| 1/I | 2/II | 3/III | 4/IV | 5/V | 6/VI | 7/VII |
|-----|------|-------|------|-----|------|-------|
| C | D | E | F | G | A | B |

You can see how the 'C' major scale above has had each note numbered, these are the degrees of the scale. When someone uses a Roman numeral as a chord, the number/numeral relates to the note that is numbered accordingly. So in this example the 'I' refers to the 'C' chord and the 'IV' refers to the 'F' chord.

I    equals the 'C' chord
II   equals the 'D' chord
III equals the 'E' chord
IV equals the 'F' chord
V   equals the 'G' chord
VI equals the 'A' chord
VII equals the 'B' chord

The beauty of this system of Roman numerals, is that it makes it easy to change the progression into another key. The designation of 'II' or 'V' is not fixed to any particular chord, it's relative to the key you are playing in.

Here is an example of a basic twelve bar blues progression shown as Roman numerals. Eventually you will get used to thinking about it in these terms, although we will revert to the actual chords to make things easier. You can see below how the three chords fall within the twelve bars, with enough practice this progression will become second nature, just give it time.

**A Typical 12-Bar Blues Progression**

It consists of...

- 'I'    Four bars
- 'IV'   Two bars
- 'I'    Two bars
- 'V'    One bar
- 'IV'   One bar
- 'I'    Two bars

The use of numerals in place of chords may be new and confusing, but don't worry too much about it, now that we have covered the progression, and you know about the numerals, we will now be referring to the chords used by their actual names. But at least you now hopefully get the idea, which will help you understand things in the future.

For the purpose of this book we will be keeping things in the key of 'C'. With this being a beginners guide, it makes sense for the sake of simplicity. So with that in mind, we will now look at a twelve-bar progression in the key of 'C'.

So armed with this information, we can work out that for the key of 'C', the I – IV – V chords will be... C – F – G. Below is an example of a fairly typical but basic 12-bar blues chord progression, shown now as chord in the key of 'C'.

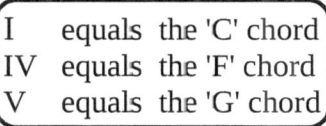

| I | equals the 'C' chord |
| IV | equals the 'F' chord |
| V | equals the 'G' chord |

**A Typical 12-Bar Blues Progression**

As you can see, there are four bars of 'C' which changes to the 'F' for two bars and returns back to the 'C' for two more. At this point it moves to the 'G' chord, but only for one bar as it then drops to the 'F' for one bar, and then finishes back where it all began with two bars of 'C'.

Although it's only twelve bars long and has but three chords, it might help you to remember the chord progression by breaking it down into three smaller sections of four bars. Not only because smaller chunks are always easier, but also because the feel of the music does kind of have three separate acts, in a sense at least.

**Twelve-Bar Split Into Three Sections**

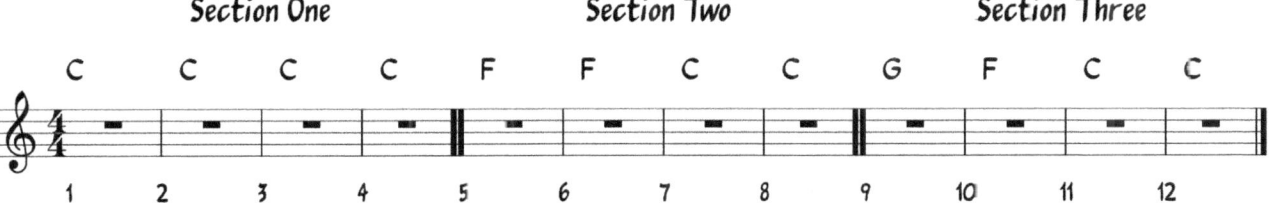

Initially at least that's all there is to it, not too hard to remember, although the trick to such styles of playing is that these have to become completely internalized and recalled/used without thought, but that comes with practice.

Next up, we'll start with the left-hand. The traditional style of rock 'n' roll we look at here is influenced heavily by the blues, with a large use of boogie-woogie type bass-lines. You may hear people talk about left and right-hand independence, and here it's important to treat the left and right hand separately. Always practice the left-hand separately until it has a degree of independence, from thought and so from the right hand.

# Left-hand 1

The first left-hand bass-line we'll look at is a basic walking type pattern which moves up through the major scale and back down again on the second bar. The notes used in the pattern are the root, third, fifth, and sixth of the major scale, with the root note being repeated at the top. It's a fairly standard walking-bass pattern, which was borrowed from the blues.

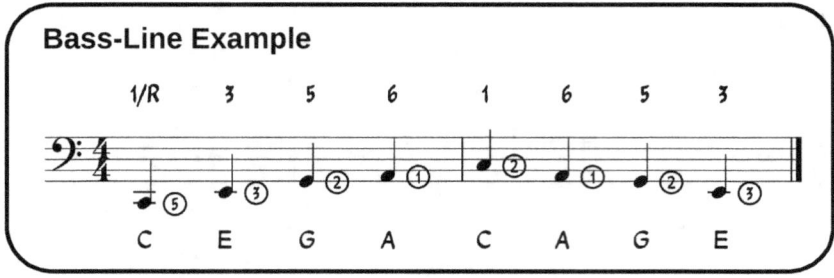

**Bass-Line Example**

## Fingering Suggestion

Start with finger 5 and move up using 3+2+1. At this point you need to cross over your thumb with finger 2, to continue up to the uppermost note before moving back down in reverse order.

Practice this in isolation over the twelve-bar chord progression below, before moving on to include the right-hand in the following pages. There isn't too much to it, but practicing the left-hand separately is an important idea to continue with, as the two hands must work independently, so initially always practice the left-hand independently by itself.

**Twelve-Bar Example**

# Left-hand 1 With Chords

Here we begin to add the right-hand using simple triads in the form of major chords. Each chord is repeated on the off-beats throughout the example.

**Twelve-Bar Example**

2 AUDIO

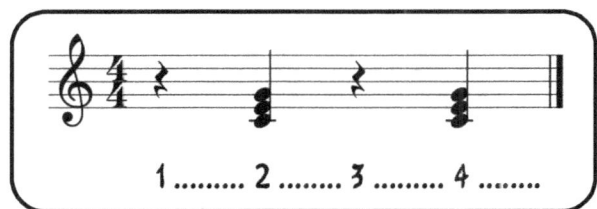

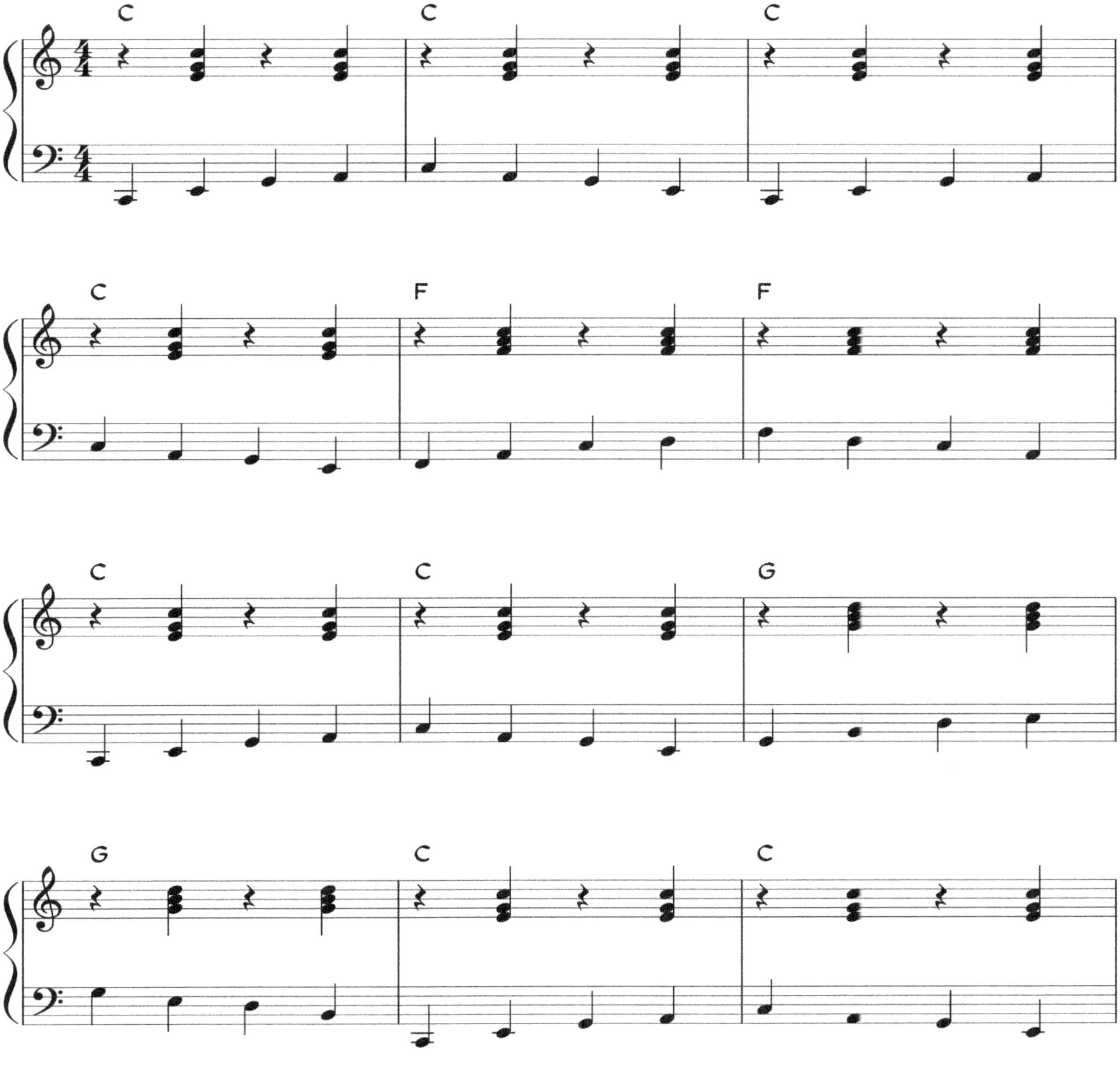

## Left-hand 1 With Chords Continued...

# Left-hand 2

Here we take the previous bass-line pattern and add a little to it. The left-hand stays mostly the same, using the root, third, fifth and sixth, but now instead of moving up to the root note, it now uses the flat-seventh. This can be played with the same fingering as before.

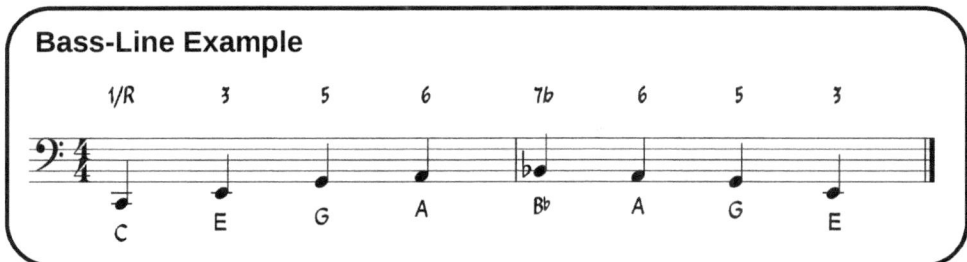

Practice this in isolation over the twelve-bar chord progression below, before moving on to include the right-hand in the following pages.

**Twelve-Bar Example**

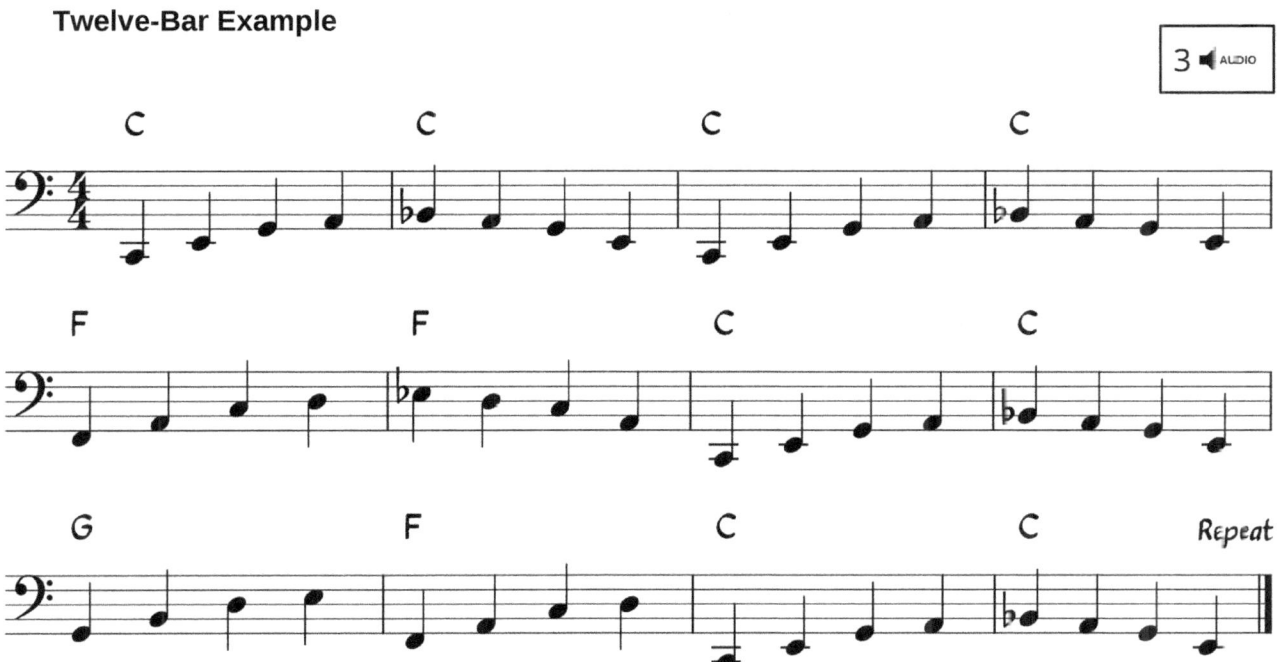

Note how the seventh isn't used in bars nine and ten this time. This is because bar ten has changed to the **IV** chord, so the '**G**' and '**F**' chords only have one bar each, so not allowing enough room to develop the pattern fully.

# Left-hand 2 With Chords

10

Left-hand 2 With Chords Continued...

# Left-hand 3

Taking the same theme as before, here the second bar of the pattern is altered somewhat, and now has you alternating between the fifth and the sixth notes.

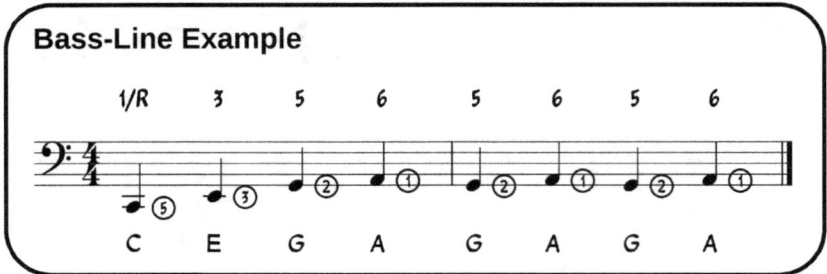

### Fingering Suggestions

Start with finger 5 and move up using 3+2+1. At this point, you just alternate between 2 and 1 for the top notes in the second bar.

Practice this in isolation over the twelve-bar chord progression below, before moving on to include the right-hand in the following pages. Make sure you can play it comfortably without too much thought.

### Twelve-Bar Example

# Common Chords

There are three chords that we will be using a lot, which you must be familiar with. These aren't overly complicated, all being major chords with an added additional note.

The **SIX** chord is just a major chord with the sixth added.

The **SEVEN** chord is just a major chord with the seventh added. (Note that this is the dominant seventh or flat-seventh, not the major seventh).

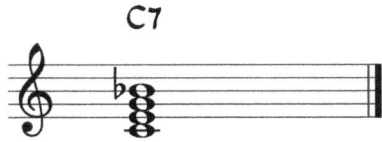

The **NINE** chord is a major chord with the seventh and ninth added. The ninth is the same as the second, it's merely been counted on above the seventh.

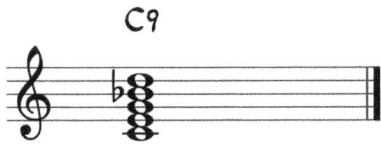

Note that the nine chords are normally played without the root note, which keeps it at a more practical four notes, rather than a pretty impossible five, which is a bit tricky for one hand. Below you have a **C9** chord shown in different inversions.

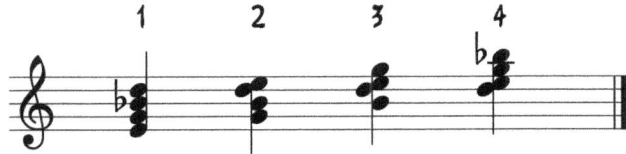

# Rock The Walk

Rock The Walk Continued...

# Alternate Rocking

16

Alternate Rocking Continued...

# Repetitive Eighths

With rock 'n' roll being rather loud (one of the early styles to adopt the use of amplified electric guitars) means the piano can have issues being heard in a full band situation. Being up against both drums and electric guitars, the style evolved to forego more delicate techniques and develop into a more aggressive repetitive form. This sees the repetitive eighths seen in the chopping style left-hand extend into the right-hand.

This can be seen in various forms, from full chords to different intervals like thirds or fifths, some examples of which are shown below.

**Full Chords**

**Fifth Intervals**

**Third Intervals**

**Sixth Intervals**

**Timing/Count**

1 .......+...... 2 ......+........ 3 ......+........ 4 ......+......

# Walking Eighths

# Left-Hand 4

This pattern is a standard within blues, boogie-woogie, and rock 'n' roll. The difference here is that it's often played straight rather than with a shuffle/triplet feel found in most blues/boogie music. With that in mind, it's played exactly as it's shown below, all notes being equal eighth notes.

It uses the root at the base, with the top alternating between the fifth and sixth. Simple enough, the hard part is playing it consistently bar after bar at a good speed. Practice this over a twelve-bar progression like before, until you can play it comfortably without too much thought/concentration.

## Fingering Suggestions

You can use fingers 5+1 throughout the pattern, or alternatively, use 5+2 on the first group of notes and 5+1 on the second. Both have their good points, but personally I favor the first one, as although less conventional, it's stronger, which is important for this style of music, as the left-hand has to really pound it out. That said, feel free to choose whichever way is more comfortable for you, so try them out and decide what works for you.

**Option One**

**Option Two**

Practice this pattern over a twelve-bar progression like before, until you can play it comfortably and without too much thought/concentration.

**Twelve-Bar Example**

9 ◀ AUDIO

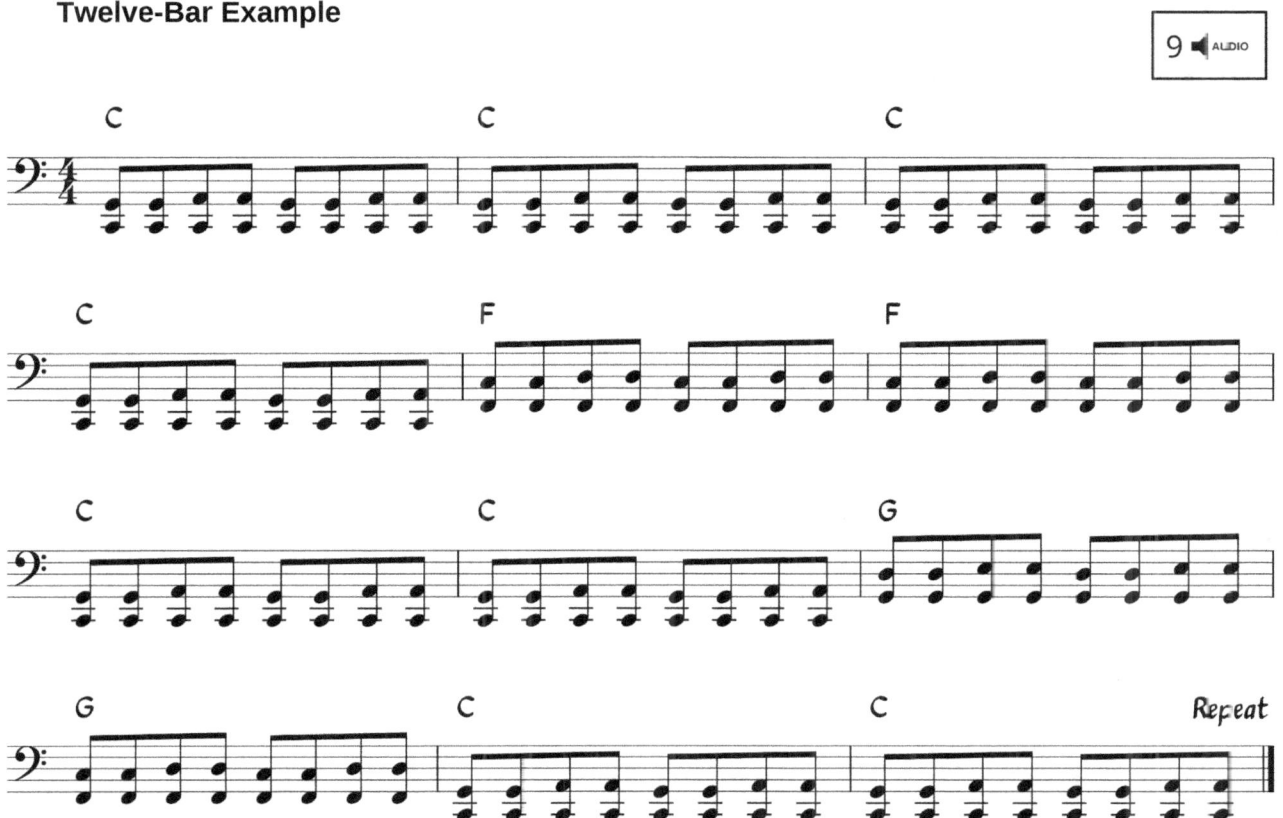

# Rock The Fifths

Rock The Fifths Continued...

23

# Root And Fifth

Quite often the entire chord isn't used, as that many notes close together can muddy the sound. When trying to be heard on the piano in a loud band situation, it helps to use a cleaner, less cluttered sound that can cut through. So here we are looking at the use of the root and fifth. As a side note, it also helps to cut through by playing in the higher registers.

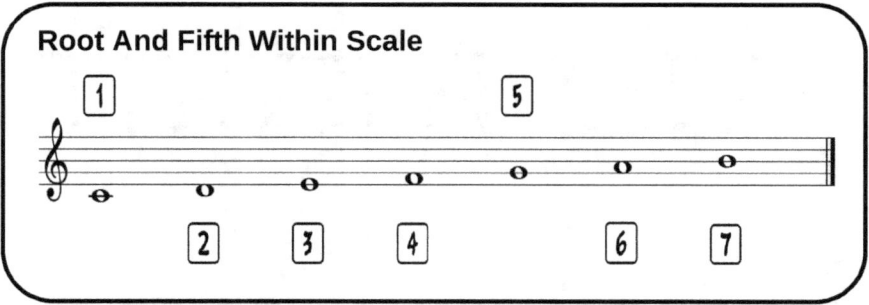

**Root And Fifth Within Scale**

Above you can see the root and fifth from the 'C' major scale, this is actually a fifth interval. If you take a basic major chord and omit the third, this is what remains. This provides a sharper sound than a full chord, and so is easier to be heard.

I'm referring to this as the root and fifth, rather than a fifth interval, as these two notes can be played in different positions, which then become a different interval. But it's the root and fifth notes of the chord that we want.

**Root And Fifth Positions**

There is a simple embellishment to these two that you can add, the addition of the flat-fifth. In the case of 'C' that will be the **G**-flat.

**Example Riffs**

# Rockabilly Five

25

Rockabilly Five Continued...

## Adding To The Root And Fifth

The flat-fifth added an extra dimension to the music by creating much needed movement, so let's take it a little further and add a few more notes to this.

**Additional Notes In Use**

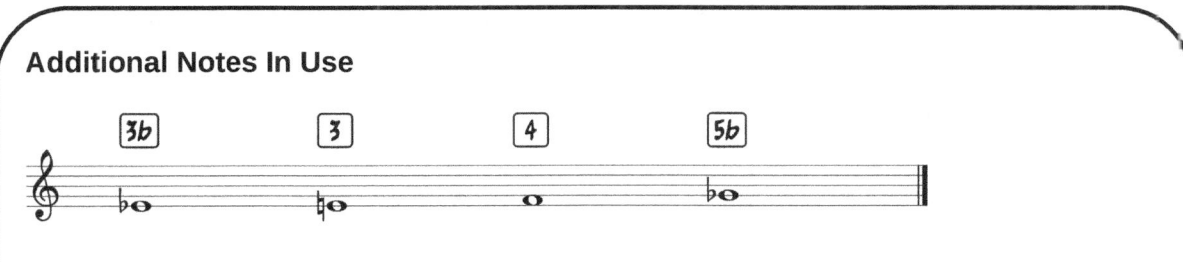

Above we have the flat-third, third and fourth added to the flat-fifth we have already used. Incidentally, this combination of notes are all from the blues scales, from which rock'n'roll stemmed.

**Example Riffs**

**1.**

**2.**

**3.**

**4.**

**5.**

# Rocking The Eighths

28

Rocking The Eighths Continued...

29

## Rocking The Eighths Continued...

# Thirds

A third refers to a third interval, two notes that are three steps apart within a scale. Below they are grouped together, although they don't necessary sound good when all played in order, as it includes thirds that are minor and diminished. These get used a lot, either on their own or combined within a riff.

**Thirds Used For 'C'**

A few examples of different types of riffs that employ some thirds, intermixed with single notes (often the root, alternating between it and the thirds) and also including the odd chord.

**Example Riffs**

1.

2.

3.

4.

**5.**

**6.**

**7.**

## Runs In Thirds (Downwards)

These patterns (referred to as runs) are a run down the keyboard using thirds.

**1.**

**2.**

**3.**

# Hammer The Thirds

Hammer The Thirds Continued...

# Thirds Are Rolling

Thirds Are Rolling Continued...

# New Chord Progression

There are many chord progressions in rock 'n' roll, some that move away from its blues roots, but this next one is only a slight variation on the standard twelve-bar, and you'd have no doubt heard it many times before. You can see that everything remains the same, apart from the last bar, which changes to the 'V' chord.

**Chord Progression As Numerals**

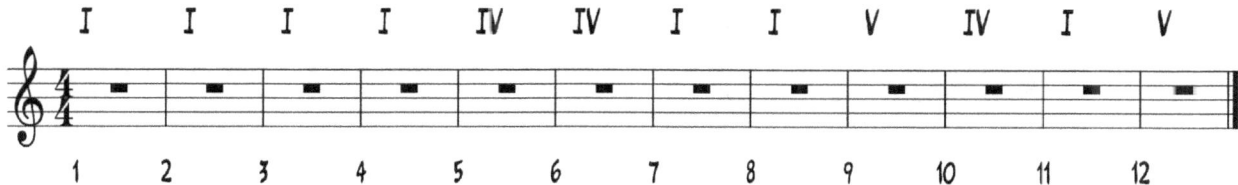

**Chord Progression As Chords – Key of 'C'**

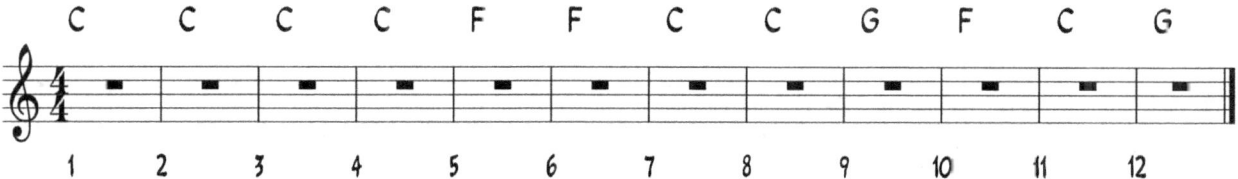

**Progression Ending**

With the last bar now being a different chord, we are highlighting the end of the chord progression, kind of like a turnaround within blues music, but simplified and in this case only covering one bar. It signifies the end of the progression and prepares you for the next one.

**Example Patterns**

# Rocking The Fives

38

Rocking The Fives Continued...

# Slurs/Grace Notes

A great technique to add life to the music, is the use of grace notes or slurs. This is where you play a note momentarily before the actual note you require. It doesn't really have a timing value of its own, as it sounds for the merest fraction of a second. These are generally used on the third and the fifth.

### Example Third

The grace note is a semi-tone below the target note. Here we have the **D-sharp** before the **E**.

### Example Fifth

The grace note is a semi-tone below the target note. Here we have the **F-sharp** before the **G**.

Introduce them to your own taste, experiment with them and play them when you feel it will enhance the music. From listening to music you will get a feel for this over time, bear in mind, that like many things in life, too much of a good thing can be too much.

### Technique

Unlike classical music where a grace note would normally be played with another finger, here the same finger is often used, sliding off from the first note and down onto the second.

Please note that this isn't possible in all keys and sometimes two fingers will be required, although this also means it's more suitable for use in some keys than others.

# Left-Hand 5

This pattern is in some ways a combination of the slower walking type bass and the more aggressive chopping type bass line. It moves up thorough the scale alternating notes with the root. It uses the root, third, fifth, and sixth notes of a major scale.

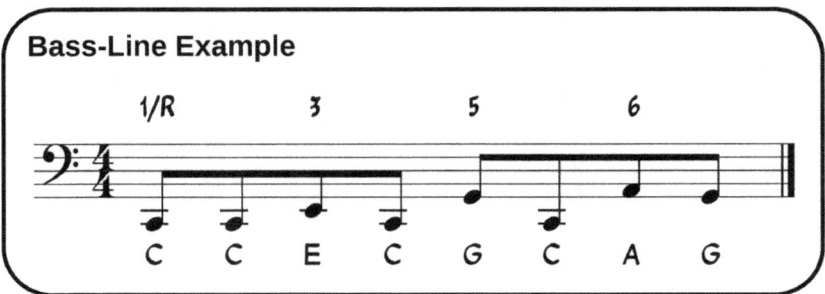

## Fingering Suggestions

The fingers you'll use are similar to the walking bass type patterns, as although this can no longer be referred to the former, it does use much the same notes, which also move upwards in a similar manner, it's just a lot busier.

Option one uses 5+3+2+1 as it moves upwards, the higher notes changing fingers while the root at the bottom remains with finger 5.
Option two is less conventional, using 5 at the bottom root note, and then only 2+1 used above for the rest of the notes. This requires more movement with the thumb, but this also positions the hand so that the bottom root note can also be played with finger 4 at the same time as 5 (yes, I said it was unconventional). This works well, as it makes the lowest root note far stronger than otherwise possible with only the little finger, and having a strong bass is important in this style. Try them out and decide what works for you, the first is quite conventional, the second is more unique to this style and way of thinking.

### Option One

### Option Two

Practice this pattern over the twelve-bar progression without the right-hand until you can play it comfortably and without too much thought. This is perhaps a little harder than the previous chopping type patterns, as there is a fair amount of extra movement than before. Once you're happy playing this, move on to try 'Rock The Keys' on the next pages, which has the right-hand added.

**Twelve-Bar Example**

16 ◀ AUDIO

# Rock The Keys

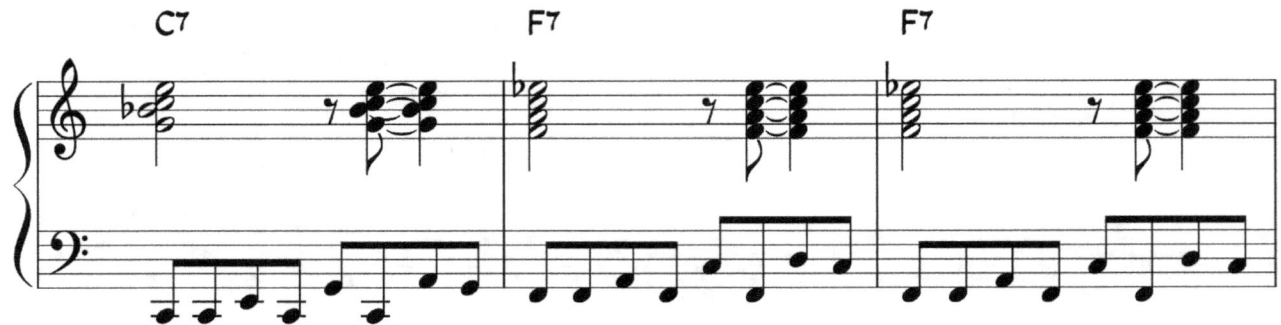

Rock The Keys Continued...

# The Glissando

A glissando is synonymous with rock 'n' roll piano. Those flashy sounding streaks of sound as the pianist runs down the piano, that the likes of Jerry Lee made famous certainly sound good, and help the piano stand out amid the noise of a loud band.

First thing to point out with this, is that in one respect it isn't as difficult as it might look. Of course that doesn't mean it's easy, but just perhaps not as hard as may first be thought, but of course like everything else in life it takes practice. Another point is it's quite physical, so you must be careful not to cause yourself any harm while doing these.

You can find them in sheet music as being notated like the examples below. Note that the 'gliss' wording isn't always included.

**Glissando Notations**

**1.**

Here the notation is quite specific as to the start and end point of the glissando.

**2.**

Here it has a start point but no definitive end.

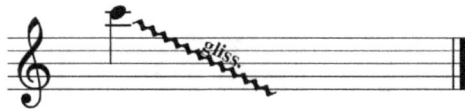

### How To Make Contact

Exact techniques between players might vary a little, and how it's done also depends on if you are moving up or down the keyboard. Just remember that your fingers are soft, and the keys are rather hard, so in order to do this effectively and safely, you ideally want the middle of your finger nails to make the contact.

### Moving Down

Moving down you will be using your thumbnail.

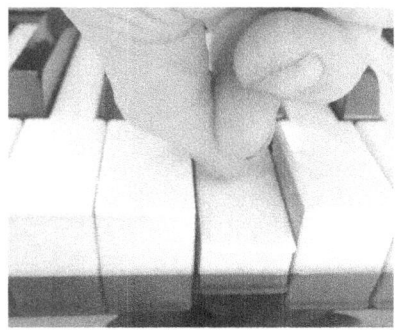

### Moving Up

Moving up you will be using your fingers nail.

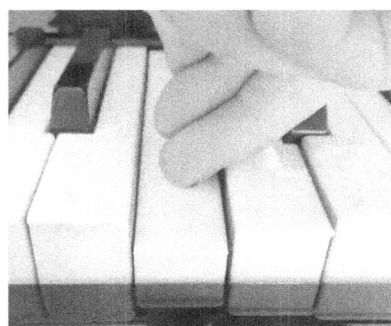

**Tips**

To play these effectively it helps to have a definitive start and end point, rather than randomly swooshing down the keys. Don't be over the top precise and fussy, but it does help it sound far more precise/deliberate. Don't be shy, these are supposed to be loud and flashy, so lean on it, make it loud and proud.

Practice doing glissando's in various positions with different start and end notes and also practice over two, three and four octaves.

**1.     Slide Down Two Octaves (C To C)**

**2.     Slide Down Three Octaves (C To C)**

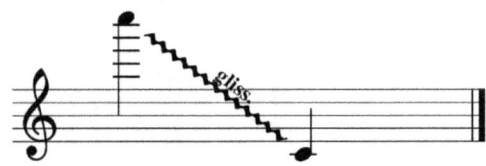

**3.     Slide Down Four Octaves (G To G)**

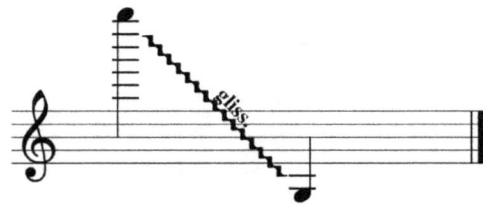

**4.     Slide Up Four Octaves (F To F)**

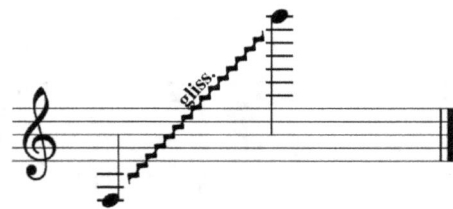

# Glissing It

# Left-Hand 6

A slight alteration to the previous left-hand pattern which sees the root note being repeated on every measure. This gives it a fuller more aggressive sound, although it also increases the physical difficulty when played at a high tempo. Naturally the fingering would remain the same as the previous version, as the notes are the same as before.

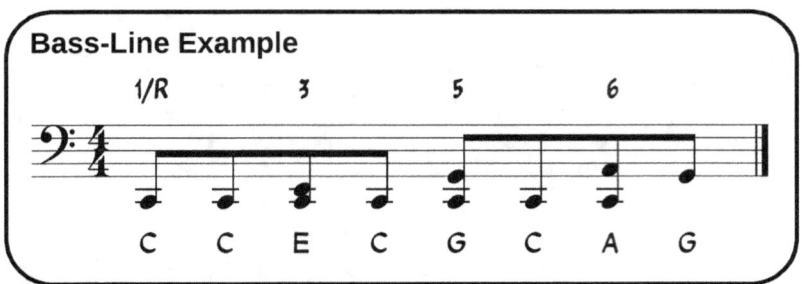

Practice this over a twelve bar progression without the right-hand until you can play it comfortably without too much thought. Once you're happy playing this, move on to try 'Just Rock It' on the next pages, which has the right-hand added.

**Twelve-Bar Example**

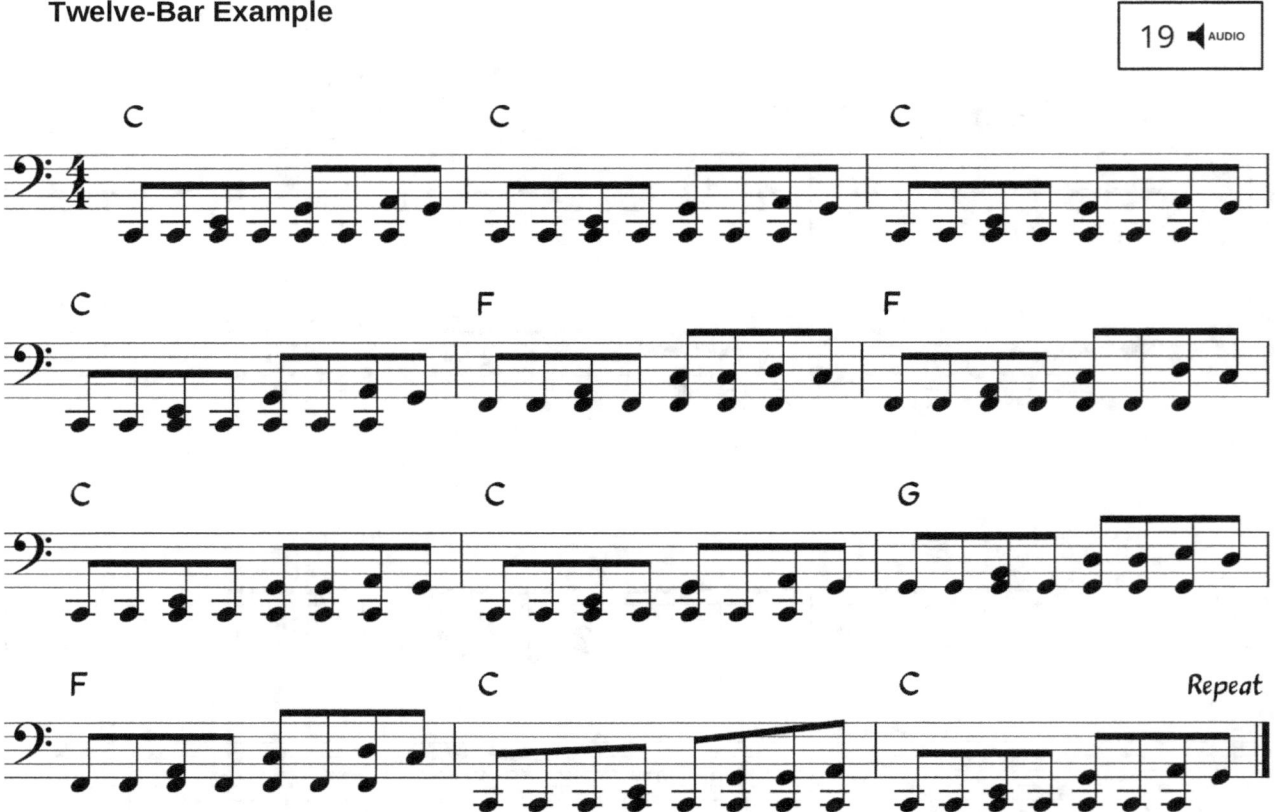

# Just Rock It

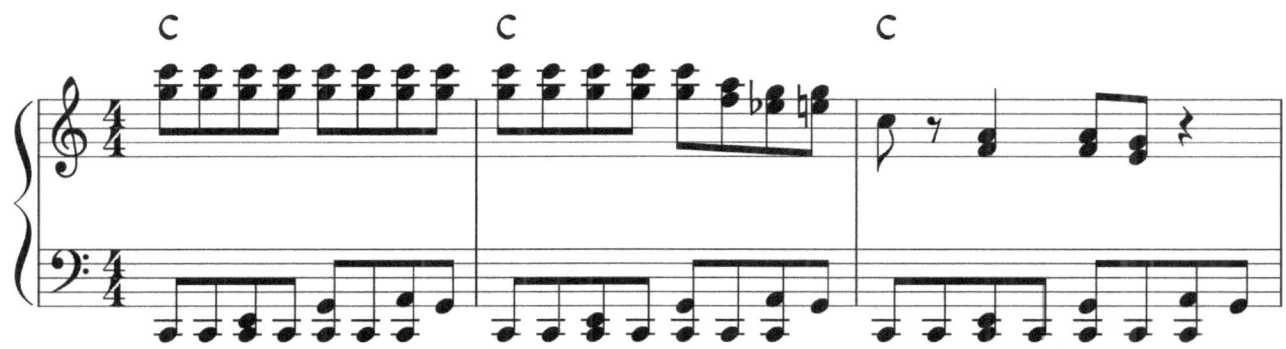

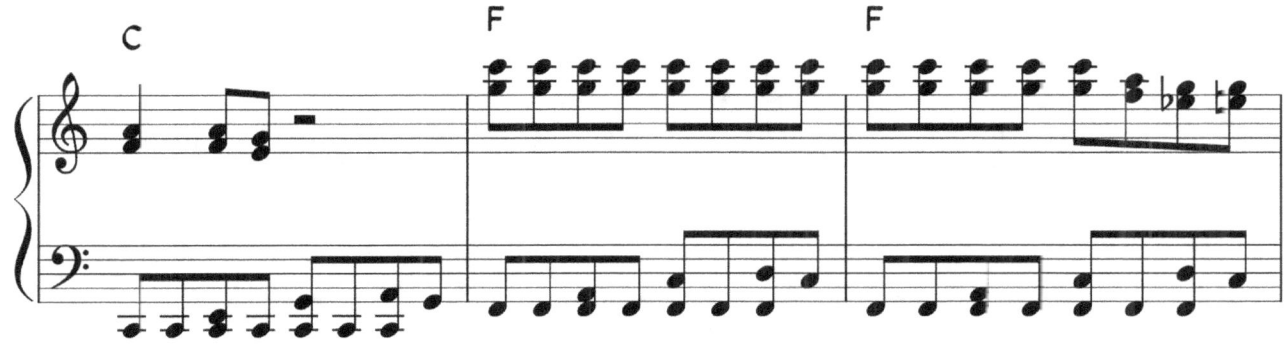

Just Rock It Continued...

# Left-Hand 7

This pattern is a slight alteration of left-hand pattern number five. It moves up thorough the scale alternating notes with the root, but it continues on into a second bar where it alternates between the fifth and the sixth. The fingering would remain the same as the previous patterns, as although the pattern has changed slightly, the notes are much the same as before and so the hand position will stay much the same.

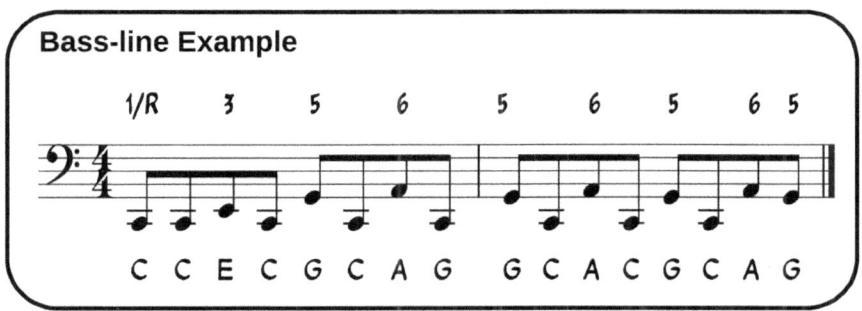

Practice this over a twelve bar progression without the right-hand until you can play it comfortably without too much thought. Once you're happy playing this. move on to try 'Seven Rolling' on the next pages, which has the right-hand added.

**Twelve-Bar Example**

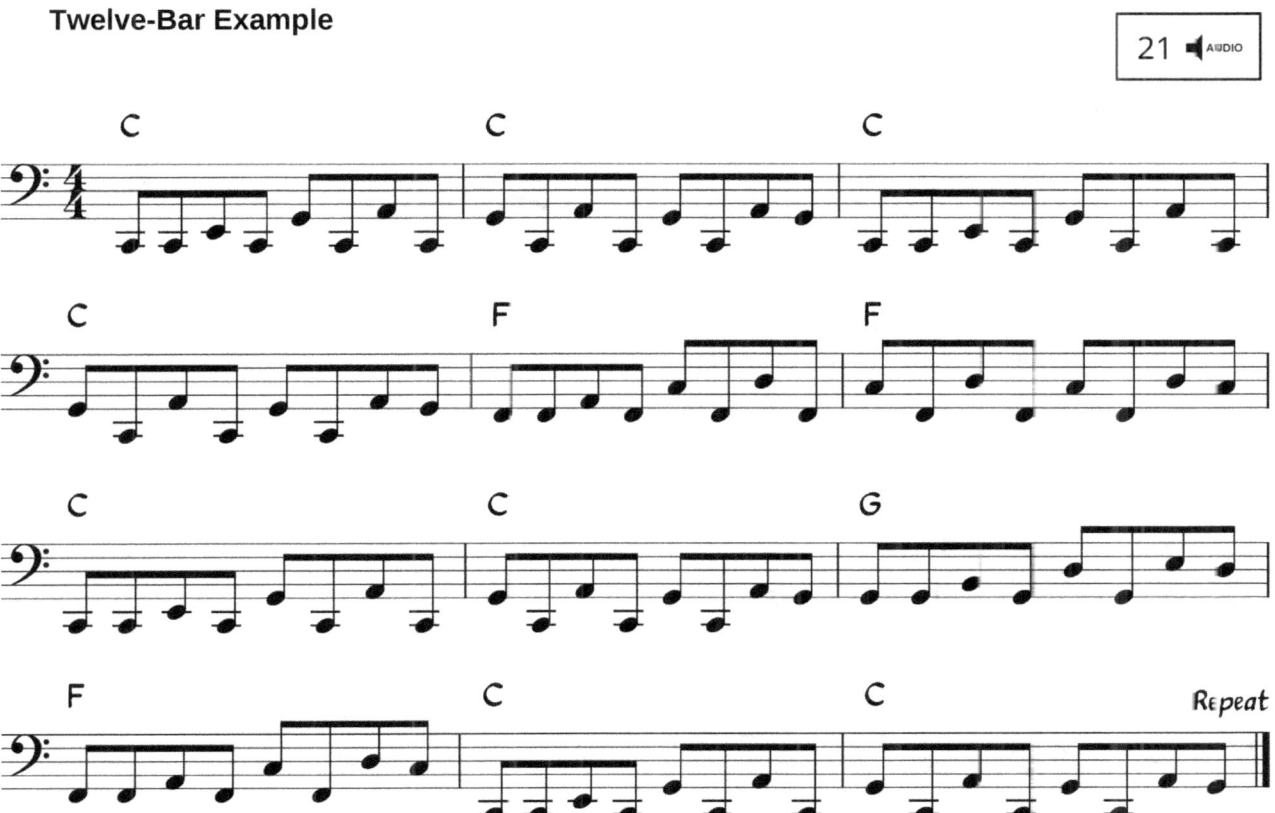

# Seven Rolling

# Shuffle Feel

The shuffle feel – sometimes referred to as a triplet feel or even a swing feel – gives a bouncing feel to the music, and is common in blues and boogie-woogie piano, from which rock 'n' roll developed.

Rock 'n' roll tends to be played straight, using eighth notes like we have used so far. But, because it developed from these other styles, there is a degree of cross over and the shuffle feel can also be heard in some music.

In some recordings you can even hear some musicians playing a shuffle feel, while others are playing straight. Like the drummer playing a shuffle beat while the guitarist is using straight eighths.

**Triplets**

A triplet is essentially a single beat divided into three equal measures. Below you can see how this works, with each beat having a count of three within itself.

**The Shuffle Feel**

The actual shuffle feel comes from using triplets, but instead of playing all three of them, the first two are tied, so you have a long note and a short note. Alternating between the long and short notes is what creates the 'shuffle' feel.

# Shuffle Left-Hand 1

This first example of a shuffle feel left-hand is essentially the same pattern as previously used in **Left-hand Five**, but the shuffle feel changes it quite a lot. Again, the fingering would remain the same as the previous versions, as it's really only the timing that has been changed.

**Bass-Line Example**

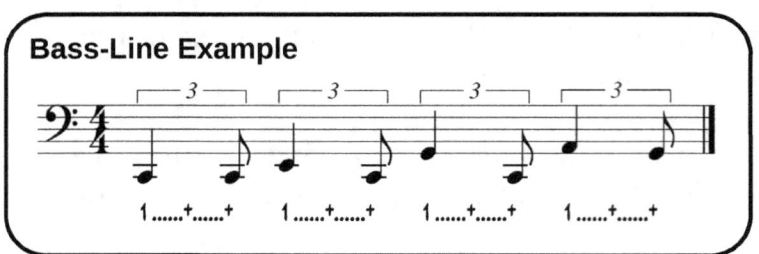

**Twelve-Bar Example**

23 ◀ AUDIO

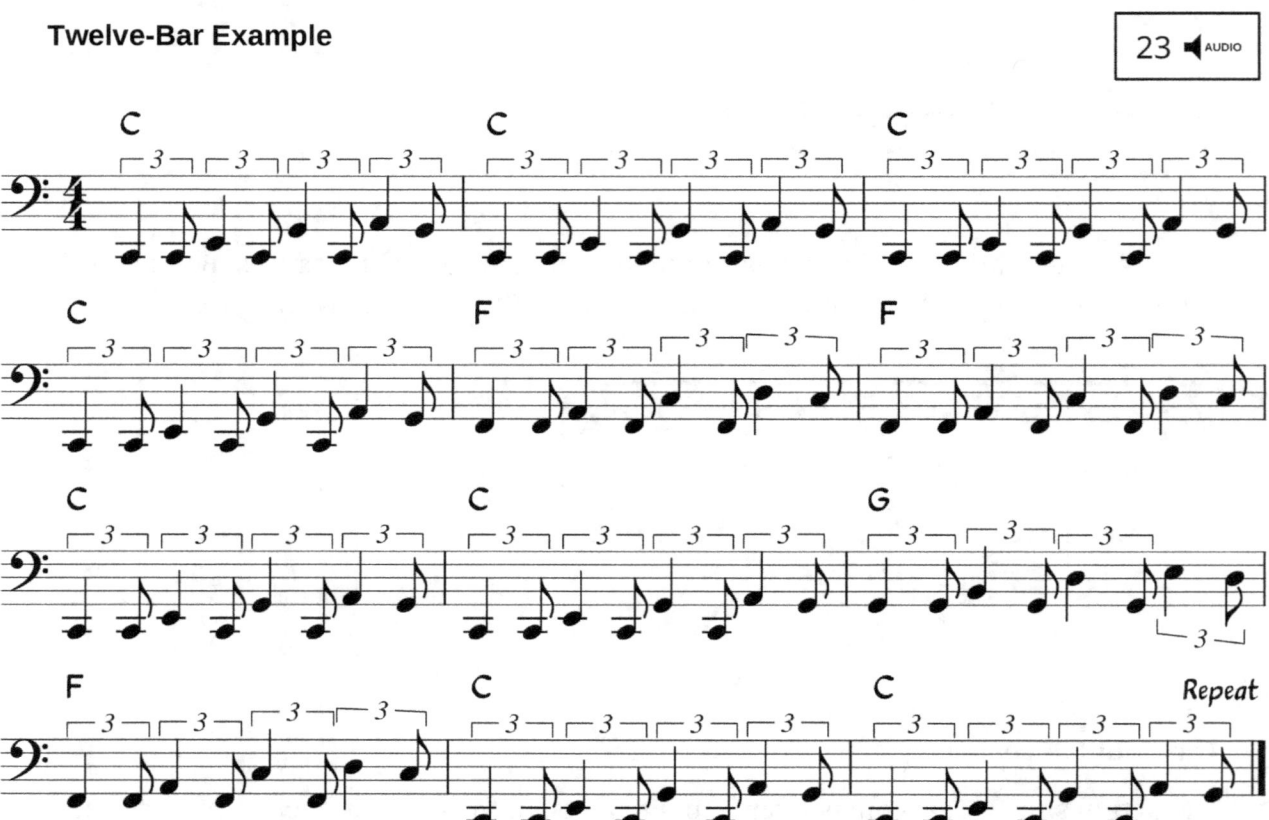

Although the first twelve-bar example below is notated using actual triplets, it's quite common to notate this using eighth notes instead, but with the symbol below denoting the true timing of the music.

# Rocking Rabbits

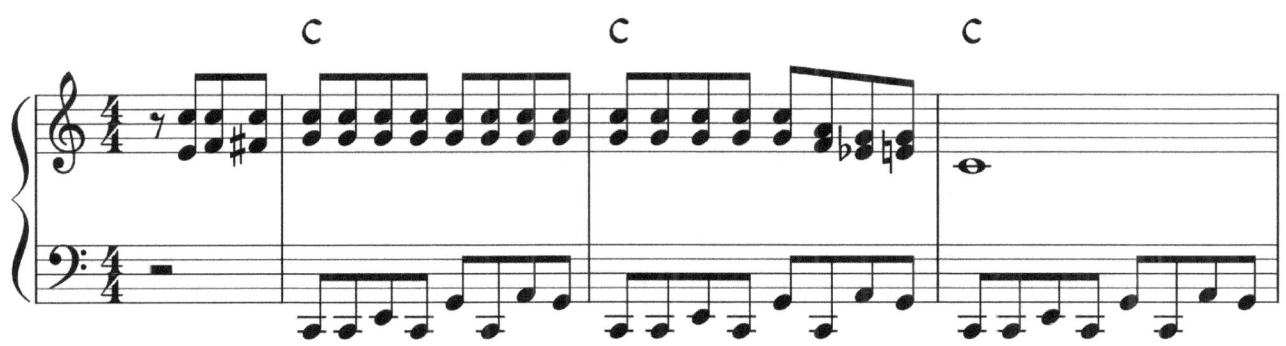

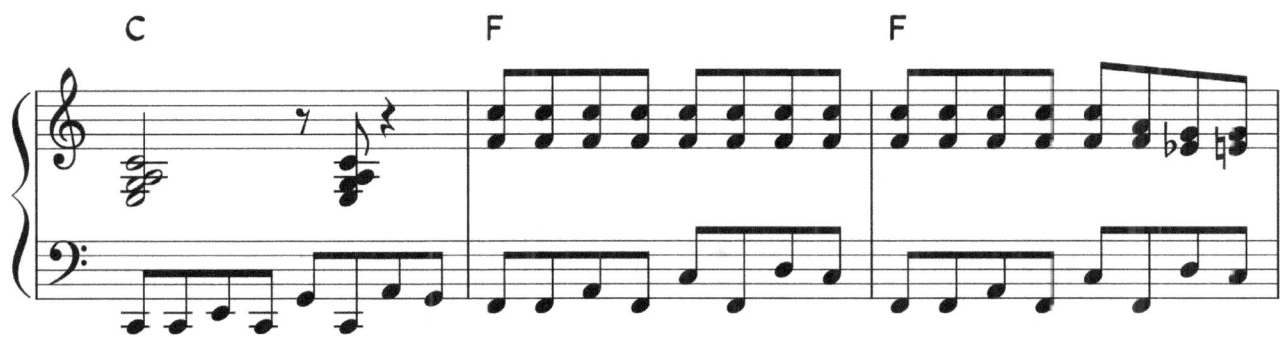

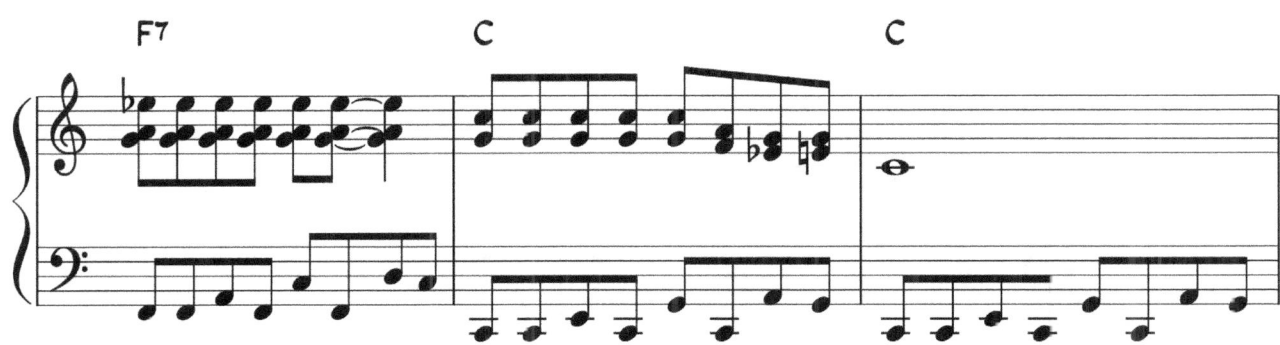

Rocking Rabbits Continued...

Rocking Rabbits Continued...

Rocking Rabbits Continued...

# Shuffle Left-Hand 2

This variation has you kind of play the opposite way around. When I say that, I mean it in the sense that the repeating root note is now at the top instead of the bottom, so it's the bottom notes that move upwards instead of the top notes.

Being in reverse, the fingering for this can feel a little awkward, so take the suggestion below as that, just a suggestion. Finger 1 needs to stay at the top, but below that, experiment with whatever you feel comfortable with.

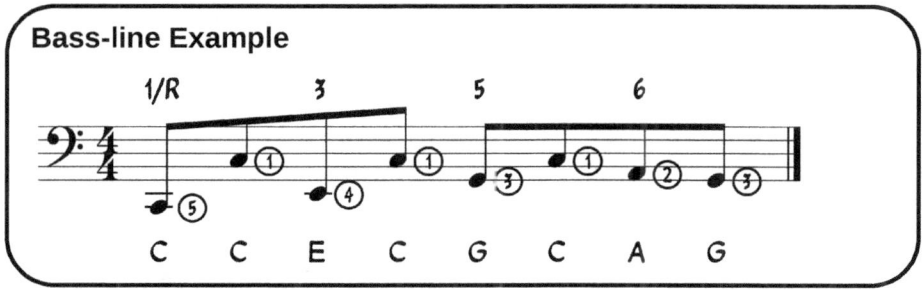

Practice over the twelve-bar progression without the right-hand until you're happy with it. Remember it's a shuffle feel. Once you're happy playing this, move on to try 'Rolling It Up' on the next pages, which has the right-hand added.

**Twelve-Bar Example**

# Rolling It Up

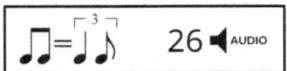

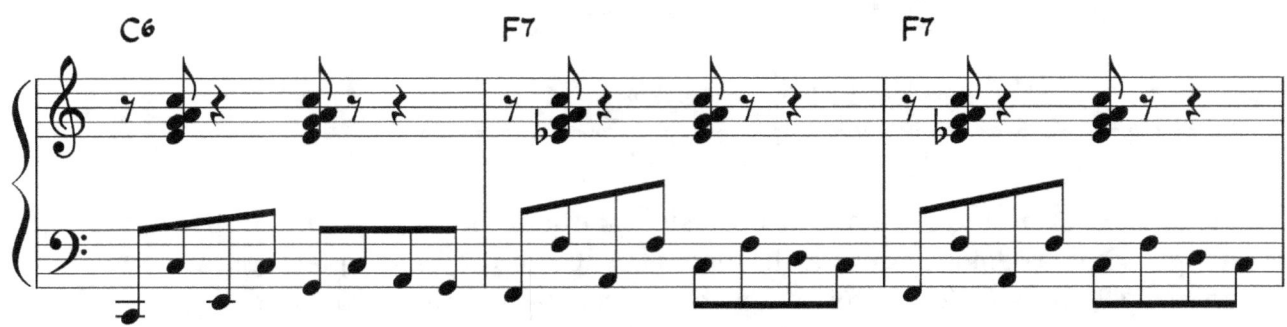

Rolling It Up Continued...

# Shuffle Left-Hand 3

The third shuffle style left-hand we have here uses the typical root, third, fifth and sixth, but this time the root note it repeated constantly throughout.

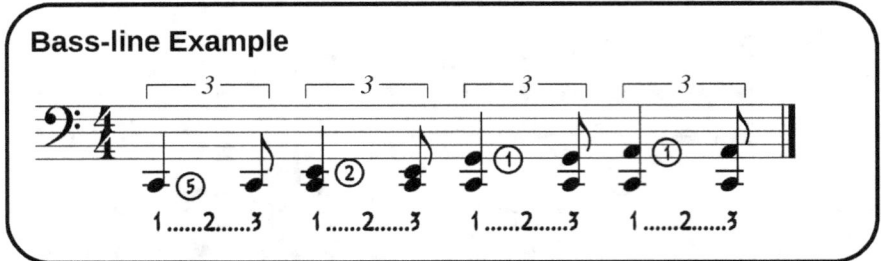

## Fingering Suggestion

Above we have used 5 on the root note, moving up to 2 and then using 1 for the two top notes. This has more movement of the thumb, but I also feel that it's the strongest way to play it. The other way would be to use 5 on the root and then 3+2+1 sequentially as you move up. While this works, I'd suggest that it isn't as strong a position for your hand/fingers. Ultimately the choice is yours, so again, have a play around and decided what works for you.

Practice over a twelve-bar progression without the right-hand until you can play it comfortably, and then move on with the right-hand with Rocking Shuffle.

## Twelve-Bar Example

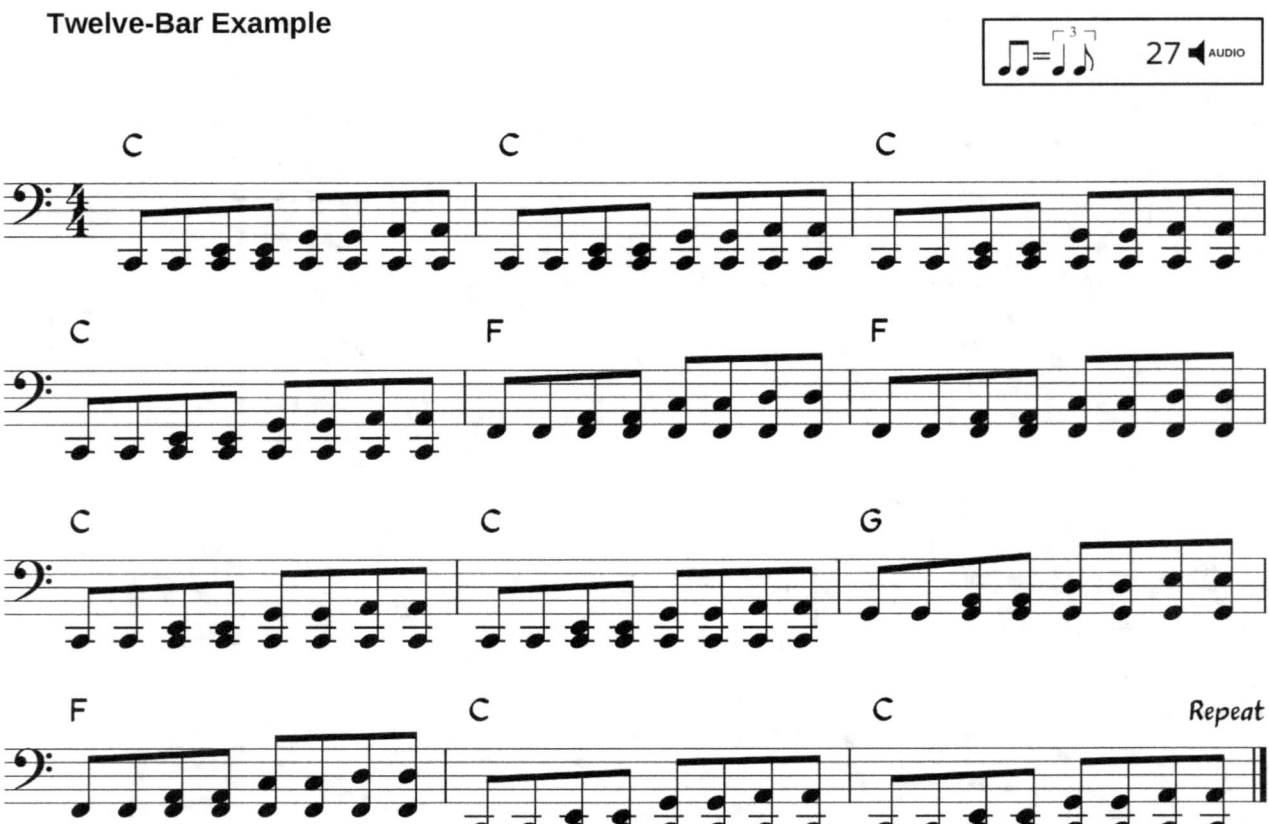

# Rocking Shuffle

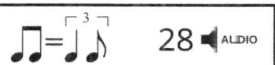

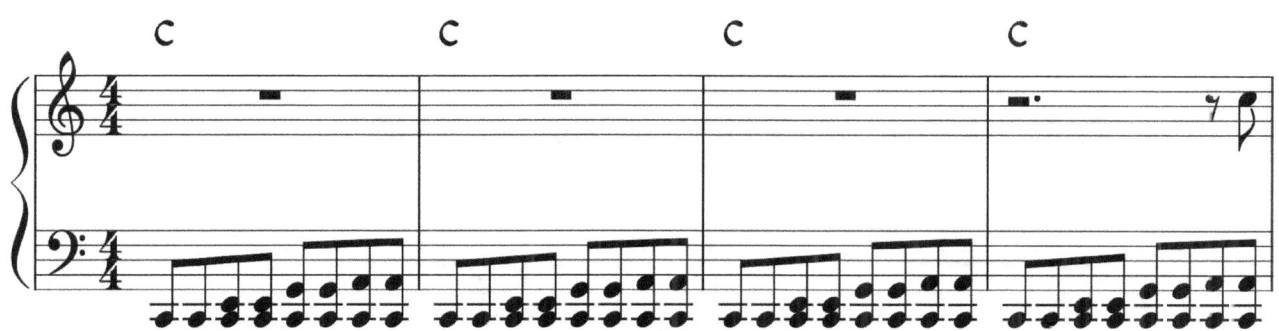

Rocking Shuffle Continued...

Rocking Shuffle Continued...

Rocking Shuffle Continued...

# Practice Suggestions

## How Often?

I will state the obvious and say that to progress and improve at anything you need to spend time doing that thing, so needless to say that the more time you spend on the piano the better you will become. But going beyond the obvious perhaps the most important thing to consider is consistency. The way our brains work means that to learn anything we must do that thing continuously as we don't absorb anything complex instantaneously, sadly. The best way to progress is to practice every day, this keeps everything fresh in your mind and constantly forces your brain to absorb the new information and skills it is being fed. You may have heard of the ten thousand hour theory? Where you need to do the thing in question for ten thousand hours to become an expert? Well, who knows what the exact amount it, it would obviously vary from person to person, but it reminds us that it takes time and hard work to become good, so... how good do you want to become?

Of course extremes aren't possible for everyone, it's fine for professional musicians who play for a living but for many, they don't have the same time, inclination, or necessity. But of course your practice doesn't have to be for hours and hours every day, when you can and want to fit in a long session, then great, do so, but don't feel as if you have to. But if you can fit in ten or twenty minutes a day regularly then do it, as it will make a big difference in the long term. So if you have ten minutes before leaving for work, waiting for a takeaway or a taxi, whatever, sit down and make use of the time, in the long term you will be happy you did. Just remember, consistency wins the game every single time.

## Physicality

This style of music is quite physical and hard on the hands, so bear in mind that it takes time to build up the endurance and strength in your hands to play this style effectively. If you ever feel any discomfort, stop and have a rest from playing.

## Sleep

Sleep isn't something you would necessarily link to playing an instrument, but the time you spend sleeping is the time when the piano skills you have been working on are processed by the brain. So, getting a good nights sleep makes a big difference to learning, remembering and so absorbing what you have been working on.

## Metronome

Using a metronome while practicing is highly recommended. The use of one will really help with keeping the timing tight throughout and also when learning a part that has timing you are unaccustomed to. When I say metronome, use whatever you have, which may literally be a mechanical metronome, one on a digital instrument or even an app on your phone. Playing along to a drum beat backing is also an option, perhaps even preferred for this type of music in fact. Or further to this even, put on some real music from whatever artist you like and play along, this really helps a lot in getting the feel of the music right.

## Listen To The Music

To really get the feel of any style of music, it is vital that you listen to it as much as possible. This really helps you internalize the sound, which in turn will help enable you to recreate it on the piano. There really is no substitute for this, no amount of sheet music can portray the feel of a style of music as well as listening to it can. So listen to it at home, in the car or when out for a walk or a jog, listen, listen and listen. It's not just for enjoyment, you are also learning at the same time.

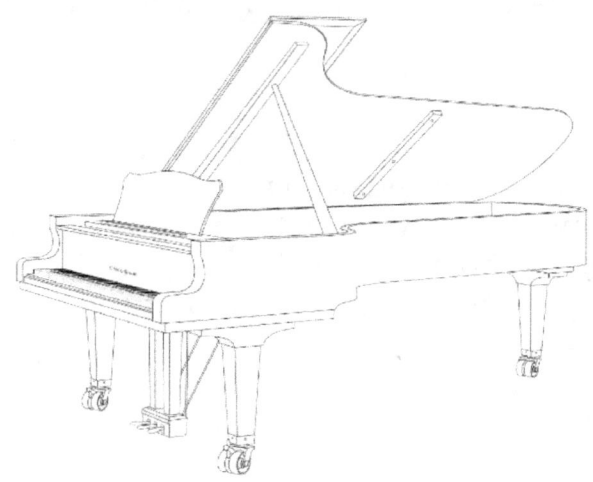

# Downloadable Audio

Audio files based on the examples within the book are available to download from the website in MP3 format, simply follow the instructions below.

To access and download the MP3 audio files,
simply visit the website...

**www.tylermusic.co.uk**

- Click on audio downloads
- Select the relevant book title
- Enter the password... **rockroll886**
- Click on the download icon

Once downloaded, please save them for future use.

## Downloadable Audio Files

1) Left-Hand 1
2) Left-Hand + Chords
3) Left-Hand 2
4) Left-Hand 2 + Chords
5) Left-Hand 3
6) Rock The Walk
7) Alternate Rock
8) Repetitive Eighths
9) Left-Hand 4
10) Rock The Fifths
11) Rockabilly Five
12) Rocking The Eighths
13) Hammer The Thirds
14) Thirds Are Rolling
15) Rocking The Fives
16) Left-Hand 5
17) Rock The Keys
18) Glissing It
19) Left-Hand 6
20) Just Rock It
21) Left-Hand 7
22) Seven Rolling
23) Shuffle Left-Hand 1
24) Rocking Rabbits
25) Shuffle Left-Hand 2
26) Rolling It Up
27) Shuffle Left-Hand 3
28) Rocking Shuffle

# *Tyler* music.co.uk

For further piano books (including spiral bound editions)
sheet music and information on blues
and boogie woogie music
visit the website at...

## www.tylermusic.co.uk

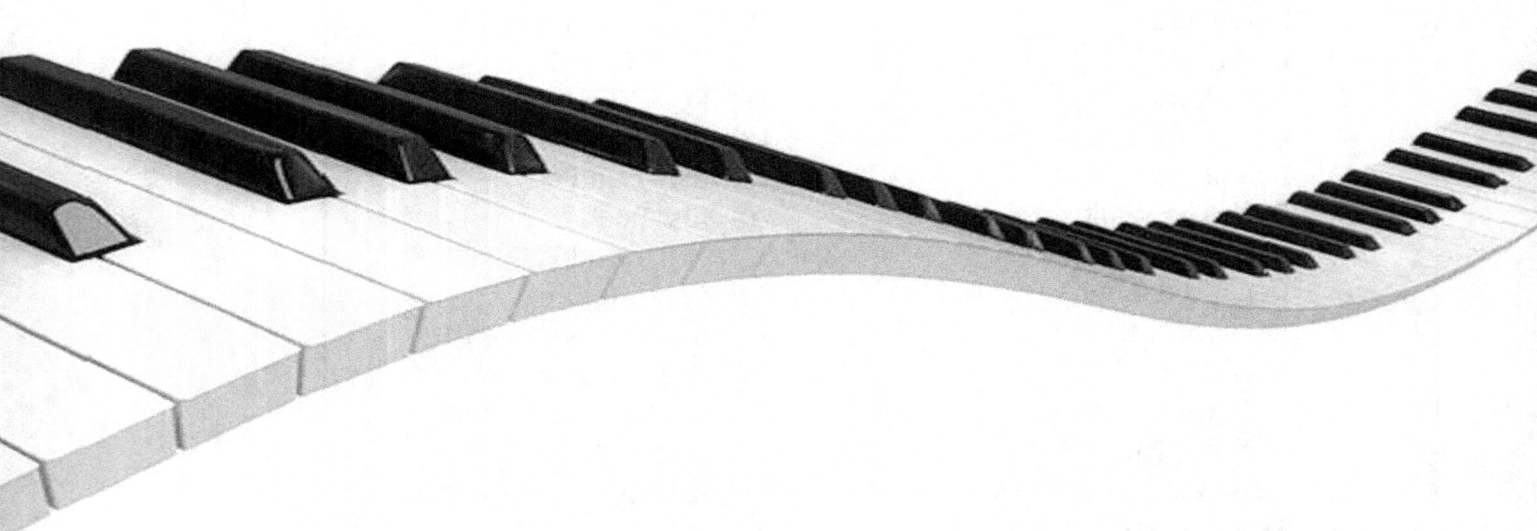

**Follow us on Facebook for updates
and information on latest releases.**

# Also Available

**Improvising Boogie-Woogie Vol. One**

Learn to play boogie-woogie like the best of them. If you want to play boogie like Albert Ammons, Axel Zwingenberger or Jools Holland then this is the series for you. The first volume in a series of books to teach boogie-woogie piano, from the basics to more advanced techniques and everything in-between, this will give you the help and material you need.

**Improvising Boogie-Woogie Vol. Two**

The ultimate guide to playing boogie-woogie continues with volume-two, adding more left-hand patterns and right-hand riffs, including aspects like the walking-bass pattern, a little stride, rolling chords, using tenths and more complex rhythmic ideas.

**Improvising Boogie-Woogie Vol. Three**

The ultimate guide to playing boogie-woogie continues with volume-three, adding even more left-hand patterns and right-hand riffs to the series. Looking at the use of thirds and sixths, the use of scaler other chord progressions how such riffs are created and how to begin to create your own.

**Improvising Boogie-Woogie: The Complete Edition**

All three volumes in one edition. Available as perfect bound and spiral bound (spiral available through the website only). Learn to play boogie-woogie like the best of them. If you want to play boogie like Albert Ammons, Axel Zwingenberger or Jools Holland then this is the series for you. From the basics to more advanced techniques and everything in-between.

### Easy Boogie-Woogie Vol.1   For Beginners

Easy boogie-woogie takes the beginning boogie pianist through their first steps into the timeless style. It covers the basics with easy to understand clear explanations and includes example pieces throughout that start off easy and gradually increase in difficulty while adding extra elements. With downloadable audio,why not start learning boogie-woogie today.

### Easy Boogie-Woogie Vol.2

This second volume of Easy Boogie-Woogie follows on from the first one, taking the beginning boogie player a step further again. New ideas and concepts are introduced along with many examples and explanations throughout. Bigger and better than ever. With downloadable audio to help you along, it's the perfect way to continue your boogie-woogie journey.

### Easy Blues Piano   For Beginners

Learn to play the blues with this beginners guide for the piano. It covers the very basics of the blues, introducing the various elements that create the twelve-bar blues sound. It starts off easy, so even a relative beginner can dive in, and gradually introduces new ideas. With downloadable audio,why not start learning blues today.

### Easy New-Orleans   For Beginners

Learn to play that unique style of blues piano from New Orleans, the style of Dr John, Professor Longhair and James Booker to name but a few. Covering everything from chord progressions and left-hand bass patterns and introducing the all important New-Orleans rhythm.

### Piano Blues Scales

The ultimate guide to learning the blues scales for the piano. The scales are clearly shown and explained in all keys for both major and minor scales along with fingering suggestions. But it doesn't stop there, here we go further and include ideas like the combined scales and methods of how to practice and use the scales in a more musical and practical real world fashion.

### Bite Sized Specifics – Blues Piano/Walking-Bass

Learn to play the walking-bass for blues piano with the first in a series that concentrates on specific aspects of blues piano. Concentrating on the left-hand, it looks at what the walking-bass is, how it is created and various ways to which you can employ it in a blues environment.

### Bite Sized Specifics – Blues Piano/Stride-Piano

Learn to play blues piano using the left-hand stride style. The second in a series that concentrates on a specific aspect of blues piano. Concentrating on the left-hand, it looks at what stride is and how it is created and various ways to which you can employ it in a blues environment.

### Bite Sized Specifics – Blues Piano/Right-Hand Vol.1

Learn to play blues piano with the third in a series that concentrates on specific aspects of blues piano. Concentrating on the right-hand, it concentrates on the important aspect of comping, which is the more rhythmic side of blues with an emphasis on the important use of chords and repetitive patterns/riffs that form the backbone of the music.

**Tyler Music – Blues & Boogie-Woogie Piano**